Letters to Jesus

Devotionals from the Heart

by Pamela Gallegos

Copyright © 2025 by Pamela Gallegos
All rights reserved.
No portion of this book may be reproduced in any form without written permission from the publisher or author, except as permitted by U.S. copyright law.

Dedication

I want to dedicate this book to my family and friends who have always been there for me. Listening to my hopes and dreams, year after year. For praying for me and giving me wise counsel. I am beyond grateful for each of you.

Thank you to my sons, John and Noah. You have always been my biggest driving force to do well in this life. To my mother Alice - nothing can take place without your unconditional love and all your prayers. A huge thank you to my sister-in-Christ, Cindi. You see, she was a witness on the day that God confirmed that He has called me to write. I am grateful for her loving reminders and friendship.

This dedication would not be complete without mentioning my bestie Carmen and her parents, Mr. & Mrs. Gil. Carmen invited me to church when we were around 11 or 12 years old. That is when I truly met Jesus for the very first time. Thank y'all for taking me to church!

Table of Contents

Introduction 5
Letter 1 6
Letter 2 9
Letter 3 12
Letter 4 15
Letter 5 17
Letter 6 19
Letter 7 22
Letter 8 24
Letter 9 26
Letter 10 28
Letter 11 30
Letter 12 32
Letter 13 35
Letter 14 38
Letter 15 41
Letter 16 44

Introduction

Dear Child of God,

I want you to know that I have taken some of my most personal conversations with God and decided to share them with you. Let me tell you why. I love to write. I love to journal. However, I'm an extremely private person. God knows this about me. He knew this would make me uncomfortable. Yet, He called me to it anyway. To be vulnerable and share. Each letter is my heart poured out on paper. I'm trusting in the Lord and His plan.

I turned these letters into prayers. At the beginning of each letter, you'll find a scripture to read before beginning the prayer. I encourage you to ready your heart. Be open to hearing from God and open to what He wants to show you. Read the scripture. Look it up in the Bible so you know where it's located. There is a mixture of scripture from the Old Testament and New Testament. If you can, say the prayers out loud. Change words. Insert names. I've added a little "food for thought" and a space for you to make your own journal entry. Write out your own prayer or just make notes. Make these your own!

I believe it is no accident that you are holding this devotional in your hands. God is waiting to hear from you. He wants you to know how much He loves you and that He is always there.

Pamela

Daily Scripture

⁶ Be anxious for nothing, but in everything by prayer and supplication, with thanksgiving, let your requests be made known to God; ⁷ and the peace of God, which surpasses all understanding, will guard your hearts and minds through Christ Jesus.
Philippians 4:6-7 (NKJV)

Letter 1

Good morning Lord,

Today I am thinking of the future. What will it be? What does it look like? What is Your plan for my life?

Father. You know the desperation in my heart to live a life that You have intended for me. From the smallest things, to the biggest. I want to be an early riser and begin my days with You. Thanking You for all You have blessed me with. Never leaving my side and encouraging me as the worries of the day run through my mind.

I see myself as an entrepreneur for the Kingdom of God. My future husband and my children are my business partners. Making a footprint in the world of commerce. Glorifying You along the way. Using Your blessings as steppingstones to bless others and advance Your Kingdom. My heart, Lord. Oh my heart! How I desperately yearn to serve You all the days of my life! Living out Your purpose for my life. I'm thriving.

My future husband is thriving. Our marriage is thriving and each one person in our family is thriving!

Father God, I pray and ask - as I take steps towards the life You have for me and fear creeps in, remind me that I have nothing to be afraid of with You by my side. When my thoughts tell me I can't, You say I can. When I feel unworthy, You say I am. Thank you for fully equipping me for all You are calling me to do.

In Jesus' name.
Amen!

Are you starting your day with God? Are you wondering what His plan is for you? Have you started that conversation with Him? I encourage you to not just ask Him but seek wisdom and guidance from your Heavenly Father. Stay in prayer, keep your ears and eyes open and see how things will begin to unfold.

Daily Journal/Prayer

Daily Scripture

I praise you because I am fearfully and wonderfully made;
your works are wonderful,
I know that full well.
Psalm 139:14 (NIV)

Letter 2

Father,

There have been days when I struggled to be kind to myself. Days when I felt ugly. Days when I felt disappointed in myself. Days where I have said horrible things to the woman standing in the mirror. Quite frankly, I just don't like me some days. You know this because You've heard my every thought. You've seen my every tear as I pick myself apart.

Abba. Help me to see myself as You see me. I love myself but Father, I desire to master this thing called self- love. Speaking kind words to Your daughter in the mirror and having a much more positive attitude toward her.

I am grateful for Your love. For the freedom to be in relationship with You. I desire to have a stronger connection with You and continue to grow in my faith, everyday. Take me back to the beginning! Remember the day I fell in love with You? The fire I felt was like nothing I've ever experienced in my life. I want to be fully committed to my walk with Your Son Jesus. Forgive me when I fall short.

In Jesus' name.
Amen!

When you struggle to see the beauty in you, lift your eyes to Jesus. Close your eyes, take a deep breath and let His light shine down on you. Feel the warmth of His love and be reminded that you are a child of the Most High God.

Daily Journal/Prayer

Daily Scripture

6 Train up a child in the way he should go,
And when he is old he will not depart from it.
Proverbs 22:6 (NKJV)

Letter 3

Lord in Heaven,

I thank You for my children. I thank you that my relationship with them continues to mature daily. You know how much I have struggled to let them go. To let them become men. Even when I knew it was the right thing to do. It was the very thing needed in order for them to truly grow. I stood in Your way. Not letting them make decisions on their own and allowing them to make mistakes. I constantly worked overtime to cushion every fall. After all, I am their mother. I started catching them from the time they were born. Did You really expect me to let go so easily? Haha. Of course You didn't. I'm YOUR daughter. You know me better than I know myself.

Although it was a tug-of-war situation, You never became impatient with me. You let me wrestle with myself long enough to finally get it. I feel that I'm allowing them to be themselves and to make their own decisions. Sure. I will always be here for them. To lend a hand. To lend an ear. To lay hands on them and pray for them. To pray with them. Give advice when they ask for it as opposed to vomiting my advice all the time.

Setting boundaries with others was a struggle for me. I'm just now realizing that I had no boundaries with my sons. My vision was quite muddy. Lord, thank You for making me aware of this. Thank You for the family and friends who lovingly helped me see what I could not. No boundaries in my own life were causing stress and anger. The very things I was creating for my boys.

Honestly, there are still many times when I want to have that control. Then the Holy Spirit gently reminds me to hold my tongue. Thank You for this Father. Thank You for helping me to let go. My relationship with each of them is better because of it. They are growing and becoming more and more mature. Thank You for the forgiving love of sons.

In Jesus' name.
Amen!

Do you struggle to let go? Whether it's your children or a career path or taking a step toward something that will increase your life, God will be there on the other side. As a matter of fact, He'll hold your hand while you close your eyes and cross that bridge. Trust in Him.

Daily Journal/Prayer

Daily Scripture

11 For I know the plans I have for you," declares the LORD, "plans to prosper you and not to harm you, plans to give you hope and a future.
Jeremiah 29:11 (NIV)

Letter 4

Jesus,

I've needed to believe in myself more. I've needed to see the woman that You see. The one You created me to be. The one You have great plans for.

Forgive me for ignoring You. Forgive me for allowing fear to rule me. Forgive my disobedience. I say I want to know what my purpose is in life, yet I cower away when You let me see it!

Yet, You never turn away from me. You never give up on me. Thank you Jesus for that! Where would I be without You? You are my hope and my strength. When I have no faith in myself, You lift my head, smile down on me and breathe life into me. You breathe life into my dreams. Oh Abba! Renew my mind! Give me courage to press forward.

In Jesus' name.
Amen!

What are you believing for today? What would you like to see in your future? Who would you like to see there? A spouse? A new you? Are the plans you have yours or God's? Are you growing impatient? Weary? Let me encourage you with Psalm 27:14 as it says – Wait on the Lord; Be of good courage, And He shall strengthen your heart; Wait I say, on the Lord!

Daily Journal/Prayer

_____

_____

_____

_____

_____

_____

_____

_____

_____

Daily Scripture

31 So, whether you eat or drink, or whatever you do, do all to the glory of God.
1 Corinthians 10:31 (ESV)

Letter 5

Dear Lord,

I come to you and ask you to forgive me for my gluttony. I whine and complain about my weight, yet I do many things that contribute to being overweight. What I hope for myself is to lose the weight I need to and get lean again. Working out needs to be second nature for me. Help me to mentally push myself past my limits. I want to feel comfortable in my skin and wear clothing I've always wanted to wear. Even a dress that just shows my calves! How great would that be! I want to walk taller and be more confident in myself. Loving what I see in the mirror. Maybe I'll even give myself a compliment! Help me to be more consistent in making healthy food choices. I would like it to be a lifestyle that sticks. You know I can struggle with throwing in the towel the moment I make a mistake or fall off course. Father, remind me that I don't have to be perfect. Remind me that I won't get results overnight. I have to work for them. Just help me so that I don't go back to the bad habits that do not serve me.

In Jesus' name.
Amen!

What do you overindulge in? How do you feel after the fact? Do you feel guilt? Disappointment in yourself? Take it to God. Ask Him to forgive you but also, ask for His help. He is our Helper!

Daily Prayer/Journal

Daily Scripture

3 Commit to the Lord whatever you do,
and he will establish your plans.
Proverbs 16:3 (NIV)

Letter 6

Daddy God,

I know I have a place in the world of commerce. I never would have pictured this for myself. Ever! However, I know you have made a place for me there. I've not yet arrived, so I come to You now.

Father, I believe in my heart, there are several businesses you want me to begin. I ask for your guidance, your wisdom and Lord, I ask you to open doors that only You can. I'm praying for a team of folks to work alongside me. My children. My family. Give them positions in which they will thrive. I pray we encounter those outside our walls that will contribute to the business, and I pray that they thrive as well. Set us on fire Lord! It is all for You!

Help me to work through my weaknesses. Surround me with those who can coach me through them. I'm praying for confidence in being on the phone and speaking in person. Negotiating. Having influence on those that I encounter. That my team encounters. Gaining contacts. Leads. Deals. Contracts! Help us gain and sharpen any skills required of us to advance and in turn advancing Your Kingdom.

This is only the beginning. There are many more things to come. I believe this. I'm grateful for all the years in corporate America and the skills I learned and mastered. I'm grateful to each person who taught me along the way. Help me Lord to take these skills and apply them to the new business ventures that await. Thank you for the opportunity to have retired from my corporate job. Thank you for my for my family and friends who support my goals.

Open the doors of networking and building relationships with those who You want us to partner with. On the days I struggle to believe in myself, or things seem too hard, remind me that You are calling me to these things. May I always answer Your call and say yes to You Lord.

In Jesus' name,
Amen!

What do you feel God is calling you to? Does it seem intimidating? Are you questioning how things could possibly work out? Let me remind you that if God is calling you to something, then you are already equipped. He does not set us up for failure. So, get ready! Believe in yourself. Love yourself. Keep Jesus at the center of everything. Pray about it and move forward boldly knowing God has equipped you for such a time as this!

Daily Prayer/Journal

Daily Scripture

30 He must become greater and greater, and I must become less and less.
John 3:30 (NLT)

Letter 7

Father God!

Thank You for this day. I am feeling excited! Though the day has drained me physically, I feel alive on the inside! Holy Spirit. Thank You for these moments with You. My spirit is experiencing great joy! The kind of joy that can only come from You. I cannot imagine living a life without You Jesus! I will follow You all my days. I love You. I love You. I love You. Lord, I love You! This feeling keeps arising in me. A feeling that tells me everything is going to work out. Everything will be okay. Over the next year great things are going to happen. You always wow me God. You always show up and show out.

More of You and less of me God. I give You all that I am.

In Jesus' name.
Amen!

Praise break! Fall to your knees! Jump! Shout! Praise your Father in Heaven, for He is good! How did God show up for you today? Were you expecting it? Thank Him and praise Him for it because He is worthy of our praise!

Daily Prayer/Journal

Daily Scripture

16 Therefore confess your sins to each other and pray for each other so that you may be healed. The prayer of a righteous person is powerful and effective.
James 5:16 (NIV)

Letter 8

Lord God,

Someone in particular has been waiting to hear from me. We aren't on bad terms but I haven't cared to have this person be a part of my life. However, I feel that I should write a letter to them. I'd like to say kind meaningful words. I just can't seem to form them. I come to You for help. For words. Let the pen just flow on the paper. Take control. What should I say? What do they need to hear?

I pray that when this person reads the words written, they feel loved and feel peace.

In Jesus' name.
Amen!

Is there anyone that you know would love to hear from you? It's been a long while and reaching out may seem pointless. After all, you've chosen not to have this person in your life. Except, there is a funny feeling in your gut. May I suggest that this is God speaking to you? May I also suggest being obedient? God has His reasons. Trust Him and follow through.

Daily Prayer/Journal

Daily Scripture

I urge, then, first of all, that petitions, prayers, intercession and thanksgiving be made for all people—
1 Timothy 2:1

Letter 9

Father,

I heard someone say - "Prayer is the spiritual oxygen by which we breathe." We all need prayer just like we need oxygen. Help me Father to become better at praying. To become a prayer warrior. I know there's no wrong or right way but I get stuck sometimes. I want to pray those prayers that make the devil shiver in fear. To pray without ceasing as scripture says.

Forgive me Lord for the moments when I turn to prayer as my last resort. I know it should always be the first choice.

I know it's important to be very specific when coming to You in prayer. This way when they are answered, I know beyond a shadow of doubt that You heard me. Father, please remind me that prayer isn't just about me. Those around me need prayer. My city, my community, my church, and my country Lord God. I pray for the lost to be found and for the broken to be healed. Restore relationships Father. Let those estranged from each other, come together. Let forgiveness arise in their hearts so they can take all their woes, hand them to You Father, and let go.

In Jesus' name.
Amen!

Prayer can be about anything but praying for others stands out for me at this moment. Make a list of people you want to pray for. Be specific if you can. Either way, God knows all the details. Also, remember that no prayer is too big nor too small for God. If it matters to you, it matters to Him.

Daily Journal/Prayer

Daily Scripture

12 For our struggle is not against flesh and blood, but against the rulers, against the authorities, against the powers of this dark world and against the spiritual forces of evil in the heavenly realms. 13 Therefore put on the full armor of God, so that when the day of evil comes, you may be able to stand your ground, and after you have done everything, to stand. 14 Stand firm then, with the belt of truth buckled around your waist, with the breastplate of righteousness in place, 15 and with your feet fitted with the readiness that comes from the gospel of peace. 16 In addition to all this, take up the shield of faith, with which you can extinguish all the flaming arrows of the evil one.
Ephesians 6:12-16 (NIV)

Letter 10

Dear Lord,

The enemy is on the prowl. Lurking and searching for the empty places within me and those I love. He never sleeps and the attack on our minds feels as though it's at an all-time high. But I thank you Father for the Holy Spirit. Thank you, Holy Spirit, for Your watchful guidance. Prompting and warning me of the lies of the enemy. No weapon formed against me shall prosper! I am a child of the Most High! He has saved me! He is my Lord and I am His!

In Jesus' Name.
Amen!

Do you sometimes hear that little voice in your head that tells you to give up? Why try? You're not good enough. It finds that one thing you struggle with the most and taunts you endlessly. Tell it to shut up! You stand tall and tell it who you are and WHOSE you are! Your Father in Heaven says those thoughts are all lies. Fight back! Throw on some worship music. Praise your Father and drown out those lies!

Daily Journal/Prayer

Daily Scripture

16 Rejoice always, 17 pray continually, 18 give thanks in all circumstances; for this is God's will for you in Christ Jesus.
1 Thessalonians 5:16-18

Letter 11

Oh Jesus in Heaven!

My morning was going so well. Until it wasn't. Some days are a struggle and I feel overwhelmed by all my responsibilities. My attitude was off and I was snappy with those around me. Father, I need Your help on days like these. I want to be understanding and not be a ball of frustration and anger. I want to give grace and mercy because I too need grace and mercy.

Thank You for coming in and saving the day! Lord, thank You that even in the midst of all these emotions, Your Spirit swoops in and calms me. Even when I complain, You still love on me and give me peace.

In Jesus' Name.
Amen!

There have been so many days of frustration for most of us. That frustration could be toward yourself or toward your co-workers, toward your family. Walk away if you need to and regroup. Get in a place of gratitude. Take a few deep breaths. It's going to be okay.

Daily Journal/Prayer

Daily Scripture

12 This service that you perform is not only supplying the needs of the Lord's people but is also overflowing in many expressions of thanks to God. 13 Because of the service by which you have proved yourselves, others will praise God for the obedience that accompanies your confession of the gospel of Christ, and for your generosity in sharing with them and with everyone else.
2 Corinthians 9:12-13

Letter 12

Father,

Can I stay lost in the Spirit with You? Your presence is strong. You take me to another place and it's just You and I. Draw me closer. Keep my eyes fixed on You. Holy Spirit, lead me. Holy Spirit, teach me. Bestow your wisdom upon me. Give me the courage and confidence I need to share You with others. To share what You have done in my life. To share the indescribable experiences, I have had with You Jesus.

I'm fully aware that people need to know You Lord. But I don't always think about it. Help me to share You! I pray that it will bring people to You. Use me for Your purpose. The thought overwhelms me and makes my heart beat fast. But if it's for You, I will be obedient. I haven't been in the past and missed opportunities to be a blessing and show Your love. Let me not miss these moments again and help me to stay faithful and obedient.

In Jesus' Name.
Amen!

Has God ever prompted you to do something that was outside your comfort zone? Have you ever felt the Holy Spirit stirring something up inside and you can't deny what's going on or what He is telling you to do?

Telling a stranger it's going to be okay and that Jesus loves them? Pray over someone in public? Or in my case, pay for all the school supplies for the mom and her kids in line in front of you at the store, as she had to put things back because she didn't have enough money? I was afraid it would embarrass her. My heart was racing. I allowed my timidness to hold me back. I had just received a bonus from work. I had the money. I also had walked in her shoes. I felt terrible but later asked God to forgive me. I have thought of them over the last 15 years or so. When I do, I pray for those two teenage girls who will be grown now. I think of the baby on the mother's hip who is probably in high school. I pray for the mother. That God would meet all their needs and they would have an overflow of favor and never be without. What will you do the next time God gives you an opportunity to make a move and be a blessing?

Daily Journal/Prayer

Daily Scripture

13 "Yet if you devote your heart to him
and stretch out your hands to him,
14 if you put away the sin that is in your hand
and allow no evil to dwell in your tent,
15 then, free of fault, you will lift up your face;
you will stand firm and without fear.
16 You will surely forget your trouble,
recalling it only as waters gone by.
17 Life will be brighter than noonday,
and darkness will become like morning.
Job 11:13-17

Letter 13

Father God,

I adore our connection. Especially during worship. I know You are with me always but during worship, I can feel You. As I close my eyes and lift my hands, I'm taken to another place. I am overwhelmed by the Spirit and the feeling leaves me no choice but to fall to my knees. My tears flow and I don't know why they do but it's okay because I trust You.

Forgive me if I don't show my gratitude as often as I should. But I am grateful to You Lord. Grateful for my relationship and connection with You. Thank You for being constant. I can always count on You. During the good, the bad and everything in between. You are with me.

As my relationship with You continues to grow, Lord, sharpen my spiritual ears. I don't want to miss anything. Especially on the days I struggle, and my thoughts are out of control. I need You. Help me surrender all to You. As Your Word says, to cast all my cares upon You, because You care for me.

Thank You for these moments, Father.

In Jesus' Name.
Amen!

Take time to get alone with God. Throw on some worship music, close your eyes and invite the Holy Spirit in and surrender.

Daily Journal/Prayer

Daily Scripture

13 I can do all things through Christ who strengthens me.
Philippians 4:13 (NKJV)

Letter 14

Lord,

I heard someone say that no matter where you are in your life right now, you can turn things around and achieve your dreams. I want to believe this. Yet I find it so hard. Why? I have dreams. I want to achieve them. Why do I continue to hold myself back? Do I not believe in myself?

You know how terrible I am about following up and following through. These two things are some of my greatest struggles. I desperately need Your help in these areas. I'm great at getting started but I hardly ever cross a finish line. Then disappointment follows. I want to be that person who writes their goals down and those goals actually come off the paper. I want to arrive! Jesus! I'm overdue on so many things! Or am I? Is not my time yet? I don't know what to think!

It's that time of year where people begin reflecting and taking an inventory of how the past year has gone. The month of January is flooded with excitement, hope and good intentions. Intentions. I may take a little action towards achieving the goals I set for myself. Then time goes by and suddenly those goals and resolutions are vapors in the wind. I know this too well! Jesus! Dear God! I need

Your help! I cannot continue this way. I cannot continue to look in the mirror at this woman and be disappointed in her.

Help me to believe in myself more. Help me to see myself as You do. Remove the roadblocks in my mind. Get me out of my comfort zone and walk me into Your purpose for my life.

In Jesus' Name.
Amen!

What is holding you back from the person you want to become? The person that God has called you to be. Get honest with yourself. This way you know precisely what you have to work on in order to move forward in life. Celebrate the small things along the way and keep pressing forward. As the saying goes - Progress. Not perfection.

Daily Journal/Prayer

Daily Scripture

5 For you, O Lord, are good and forgiving,
abounding in steadfast love to all who call upon you.
6 Give ear, O Lord, to my prayer;
listen to my plea for grace.
7 In the day of my trouble I call upon you,
for you answer me.
Psalms 86:5-7 (ESV)

Letter 15

Father,

Help me today Lord to have self-compassion. I have compassion towards others. I can have compassion toward a stranger. I try to give grace and mercy. After all, I myself need grace and mercy! So why, why, why would I not have compassion toward myself or have grace and mercy toward myself? How can this be such a struggle?

Jesus. Help me to become intentional about being more compassionate toward myself. To be more kind to myself. Remind me that I am human and it's okay to fail sometimes. I have failed many times. I have fallen many times. I got up then. I can get up now. Dust myself off and try again. With You, I can do hard things. With You, all things are possible. When I feel unworthy and undeserving, remind me of who I am and WHOSE I am. I am Yours!

In Jesus' Name.
Amen!

How can you give yourself some grace and mercy? What negative thinking do you need to replace with positive thinking? What can you speak over yourself so that you can start believing in yourself? Daily, I say this to myself
- I deserve more than a mediocre life. I deserve to show up for myself. I am worthy of success. I will be blessed to be a blessing. I am open and ready to receive great financial abundance, love, health and exciting new wonderful things into my life. Things that are bigger than me. Bigger than I could even imagine. I receive it. In Jesus' name!

Daily Journal/Prayer

Daily Scripture

18 "Forget the former things;
do not dwell on the past.
19 See, I am doing a new thing!
Now it springs up; do you not perceive it?
I am making a way in the wilderness
and streams in the wasteland.
Isaiah 43:18-19 (NIV)

Letter 16

Father in Heaven,

I am praying today that I will begin to move in the direction of the life story I want to tell. The story that tells - I follow Jesus. That I am walking in the purpose and purposes of my life. The purposes You intended me for. I know Father that I need to spend more time with You. Seeking You and gaining wisdom from You.

Today, I want to say good-bye to the old me and say hello to the new me. Using this first step as a steppingstone toward the next destination and the next and the next. As I think of all the choices I could consider and where they would take me; I choose You. I choose to focus on You. To walk with You and allow You to lead me where You want me to go.

Forgive me when I fall short. Have mercy on me when things get hard and I want to quit. Allow me to draw strength that can only come from You, that I may persevere and keep pressing forward.

In Jesus' Name.
Amen!

Friend. I encourage you to let go of yesterday and press forward into the life He has waiting for you. Lean into Him. Draw strength from Him. Let go and give Him control. He will not fail you.

Daily Journal/Prayer

Princess of God

You did it! You completed the devotional. You may be wondering what to do next.

Take some time to go back through everything you wrote in the journal spaces. What prayers did God answer? Did He say yes? Did He say no? Are you grateful that your loving Father said no?

Princess of God. Daughter of the Most High! My prayer for you is that if you didn't know God, you are getting to know Him. If you weren't close to God, you're becoming closer to Him. That your relationship with Him strengthens and may you understand that when you need strength, you can draw it directly from Him.

I pray you come to truly comprehend the Father's love for you. He is the Author of love. It is unconditional and constant. No matter where you are in life, no matter what you've done, no matter how far away from God, you think you may be, He still loves you! Lift your eyes to Heaven! Stretch out your arms to your Daddy God like a small child and let Him swoop you up into His loving arms!

About the Author

Pamela Gallegos is a God-fearing woman who has always had a love for writing. After journaling for so long, she finally listened to God and has begun her writing journey. The Lord said she has a lot to say, so get ready!

Pamela is originally from South Texas but grew up in Houston. She has lived near Galveston Bay for over two decades where she raised her two boys as a single mother.

One of Pamela's favorite things is teaching God's children about the love of Jesus. She serves in children's ministry at her home church nearly every Sunday with her amazing church family.

www.ingramcontent.com/pod-product-compliance
Lightning Source LLC
Chambersburg PA
CBHW070041070426
42449CB00012BA/3129